ONE THING —
THEN ANOTHER

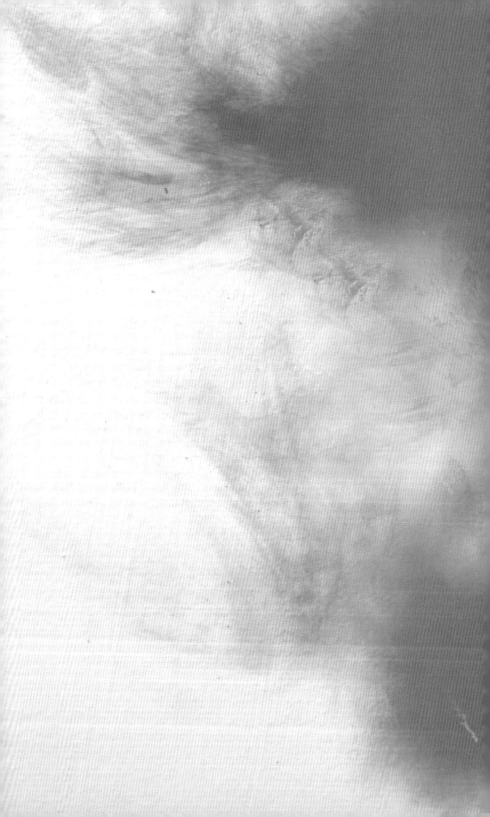

To Jenna,

ONE THING —
THEN ANOTHER

I love working

POEMS

CLAIRE KELLY

with you!

Claire Kelly

ECW

a misFit book

Published by ECW Press
665 Gerrard Street East
Toronto, Ontario, Canada, M4M 1Y2
416-694-3348 / info@ecwpress.com

Editor for the Press: Michael Holmes/
a misFit Book
Cover design: Jessica Albert
Cover image: © Shutterstock
Author photo: Rob Ross

MISFIT

LIBRARY AND ARCHIVES CANADA CATALOGUING IN
PUBLICATION

Kelly, Claire, 1984–, author
    One thing — then another : poems / Claire Kelly.

A misFit book.
Issued in print and electronic formats.
ISBN 978-1-77041-455-6 (softcover)
ISBN 978-1-77305-315-8 (PDF)
ISBN 978-1-77305-314-1 (ePUB)

    I. Title.

PS8621.E5587.O54 2019   C811'.6
C2018-905351-8   C2018-905352-66

The publication of *One Thing — Then Another* has been generously supported by the Canada Council for
the Arts which last year invested $153 million to bring the arts to Canadians throughout the country and is
funded in part by the Government of Canada. *Nous remercions le Conseil des arts du Canada de son soutien.
L'an dernier, le Conseil a investi 153 millions de dollars pour mettre de l'art dans la vie des Canadiennes et
des Canadiens de tout le pays. Ce livre est financé en partie par le gouvernement du Canada.* We acknowledge
the support of the Ontario Arts Council (OAC), an agency of the Government of Ontario, which last year
funded 1,737 individual artists and 1,095 organizations in 223 communities across Ontario for a total of
$52.1 million. We also acknowledge the contribution of the Government of Ontario through the Ontario Book
Publishing Tax Credit, and through Ontario Creates for the marketing of this book.

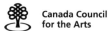 

PRINTED AND BOUND IN CANADA   PRINTING: COACH HOUSE   5   4   3   2   1

To wait staff and librarians.
To eagles, crows, and magpies.
To the Trans-Canada and Yellowhead Highways.
To Fredericton. To Edmonton.

CONTENTS

The west stands for relocation, the east for lost causes.
            —Karen Solie, "Bitumen"

Yesterday I thought winter had given up

all its images: white worn out,
utter glut of neutral.

But today, weird
mitt-ruts.
Snowbank
etchings
from kids
dawdling
their hands
to school;

overhead another storm
isn't breaking
but is moving on:

the elm-edge and the cloud-edge
slotting into each other.

As if the tree picked up
the sky secondhand,
and wears it—

a sapphire heavened hoodie
in the black and white film
of early March.

Then,
expertly,
the elm-clutch
lets loose, disrobes.
A sliver of blue expands,
becomes a sluice, a gorge,

becomes the whole
damned naked winter
flouncing down a side street
shoving her hands
knuckle-deep
in the bank.

Cool Enough to Sink a Ship

I wanna be cool the way Patti Smith says
coool.
      Take a peeler and scrape
away these tough bits. Gnarly
as a knuckle sandwich.

Oh don't croon it, baby. Siren it. Lure
my ships in.

Hey Joe,
        drop that pea shooter,
take me
        on a cruise I can't afford
and don't want to go on.

      There's me bypassing
      portholes and ice sculptures,
      eyeing floatation devices.

      There's me finagling bouillabaisse
      and breadsticks
      for the inevitable norovirus,
      the predestined crash.

Hey Joe,
        if things get choppy
and rations run out, hawk me
to the highest bidder,
             the one who knows
what's what in lifeboat soothsaying,
who isn't panicked when the waves crest.

Forget tarot cards and palmistry,
I'll show 'em their bank balance
and tell them everything's *coool*
as an iceberg
                'til tiger sharks
start circling and I crank up
these Popeye biceps, a chilly
one-two right to the gills.

STORIES MY FATHER TOLD

The way it goes:
they're skinny as he is,
long hair clotted down their backs
with different colours,
the fabric of their shirts
growing stiff, holding shape.
Two acquaintances doused in paint
meet my dad at a Montreal bus depot.

When passersby stare, they giggle,
walking from the station,
and my dad follows
looking too clean in comparison

like a masculine Alice
lagging behind two Mad Hatters,
all the way to their aslant
meantime house.
Screen door off its hinges,
smacking into the front step.
Grains of the door frame
splitting with dry rot,
wood faded grey-brown
like bad ground beef.

Inside, the fumes of still wet paint,
this hyped-up duo opens cans,
tosses their contents through the air,
all over the walls and found-couches.

A powerless fridge—
neon green and taupe.
The floor muddy,
everything running together.

There's more, one says
and hands Dad cottage-deck brown.
The fluid beauty of liquid airborne.

When they finish,
reaching for cigarettes
and warm beer,
even the toilet's
gooey and half-dried.

Later in BC,
my father sees
one man curse another,
a wand revealed
from a jean-jacket inner pocket
and tapped against a fellow
drifter's shoulder: *Today,
you're gonna die.*

That same summer my father digs
clams out of the beach
and stays—for free—
in a trailer.

Always happier telling a story
where he had no bed of his own,
when he left us
he crashed on couches
and rented fully furnished
basement apartments

while my mother bought
a new bed for herself
and repainted the walls a pale yellow
to gather the morning light.

NEIGHBOURS ARE WORMHOLES

The old lady in number 42 has the same last name
as the crescent I grew up on. She's taken to
shooing the squirrels off her lawn with her
dooryard broom and a nonagenarian's
rancour. *I'm at war with them*, she says,
is sure they're building a nest among
the off-season shoes in the vestibule
of the house across from hers. That
the no-better-than-rats will chew
through the wires to spark
the wooden structure
to blaze

.

Years ago my dog caught a squirrel and held onto the
quaking thing like he'd been looking for one all his
life, which to think of it, he had been: driving himself
against the fence like a hockey enforcer against the
boards. We thought he'd never catch one, had fun riling
him up and setting him loose to frenzy his unutilized
instinct out. And despite being three-quarters bird
dog, he'd crushed the squirrel, refusing to unclamp,
until left in my hands, this lacerated pickings taking so
long to die—I had to lay it down on the patio stones
and through tears, stop it with a brick.

SHORT-TERM DESIRES

Eurydice, in that first micro-
second, must have hated her lover
until she imagined the future
they would no longer have:

This alt-universe Orpheus bets
on the ponies with his pogey
and never plans a real vacation,
just tags along. See him mooching rides
to friends' rental cabins and forever
borrowing sieve-like tents. There's the fool
forgetting to pick up booze, forsaking
marshmallows in an opened bag
to harden back home on the counter.

And she'd have followed,
tired of nagging, tired of being
the sort of woman who spoils the fun,
though she doesn't remember
real fun anymore, just an unsettled feeling,
like spinning on a schoolyard merry-go-round
that is her own molecular structure
centrifugally yanked: herself pulled
from her very centre.

Oh, would she have chosen instead
this fantasy Orpheus who didn't check
on her progress out of the underworld,
the one who assumed she'd be A-okay?

While her synapses stretch and kink,
she thinks of him being banned
from highway driving because of his inability
to use the rear-view, pulling into
occupied lanes, once nearly side-swiping
a double-decker but only knocking off
its chrome mirror: this lifelong love of hers,
never ever willing to look back,

and her now changed, clarified
by double-sight, made and unmade
by the corkscrew truth
that she's better off snake-bit than love-sick,
love-mouldered, love-bored.

Tick, Tick, Tick Went the Machine in the Bushes

(a post-pre-post-apocalyptic poem)

*

The old saying
plump in his ears.
Red sky at night,
scrapmen take fright.
Red sky in dawn,
scrapmen are calm.

So he pitches a camp at pink dusk,
gulps a lungful of moisture,
vapour on the tongue.
Knowledge of stormpaths—
rain that's cheekbone-driven,
or that gusts between shoulder blades
and sends his rucksack a-clattering.

The man with the past in his pack,
he's a noise everyone avoids.

*

*

With each footfall or windburst,
always that discordant, rackety echo—
the world is not sweet in the end.
He remembers honeycomb sweetness
but also the sting and the sleep
of deep-breathed smoke.

What of the din? Sound so over-
lapping it seemed monolithic
but was divisible, like damn near
everything is. Down to
a single mortuary bee
bearing the dead away
from the hive. More dead than a hive.

*

*

Pull the machinery apart, pull it
apart.

The ground a tip of cursed sprocket,
of doohickey, of chrome carnage.

*

*

Pull it apart
and take it away.

Some had been told
of palaces of tile and copper
where instead of squatting
like a pure toad in the scrubland,
people sat and shat, bathed in
battery-suckled, handheld light—
the sin of mass diversion—
before having their hands
sudsed and sprayed down,
before paying alms to hot air,
palms up like a beggar's.

Mostly his old-folks jawed
through post-harvest smoke,
the smoke of tight rooms,
the hearth hot from fires ever-stoked—
constant cooking mixed with winter smells—
windows shut tight, bodies musky most days,
more than musky on others, dried herbs hung high,
and damp clothes placed near the heat
overpowering anything subtle. Until all talk
turned to good and evil, prized
and untouchable, morals and scraps.

How it was plain wrong
to owe things allegiance
you wouldn't pay
to another, your own
lover couldn't light
you up that way.

*

*

So he keeps on hauling.
On his shoulders the straps
digging in, as he carries
another sack full of smithereens,
metallic forgottens,
un-talismans,
west and away,
for good and always.

*

Sophocles's Jalopy

The father attempts to start his son's piece-of-shit car. *Got it going once, but the timing's rough.* Our bedroom funks with the reek of burning oil. *It was puffin' blue smoke. Now it won't turn over.* Annexing the driver's seat, the son gives it a go, desperate for any sign of mechanical respect. But his elder is all ever-present, gum-chewing disdain, which emanates from him like whatever it is dribbling from the exhaust pipe, smearing our shared dirt driveway. Persistent as a raccoon drawn on by the perfume of antifreeze, doesn't his kid just push the pedal down again and again while the older man gruffs: *Trash the goddamn thing. S'no good.* But the kid won't stop, maybe can't. His foot riding an arc of true need down to the floorboard, the engine's rough racket: guttural scatter pops—more alive than any car just off the lot—again and again, until his mother—a solo Greek chorus urging compromise, dealing with reality—comes out to serenade them inside. And the play, whatever it stands for, ends. No curtain call needed, the car's deep-bowing silence, an empty stage, an uncrowned king dying peacefully, the drama elsewhere.

Spring Solstice Blues

Damn eagles think they can get away with run-on sentences because they're so majestic.
   —Martin Ainsley, Facebook, 2015

This town's eagles have taken
to sending tenuous
text messages, their talons
tapping buttons
like surly DMV workers
in a bad movie.
I blame the dusk, the squirrels,
the exhaust-stained snow.
Drab dinner near
invisible, uncatchable.

Today, as I'm returning books
to the librarian whose eyebrows
tilt like art-deco awnings,
my phone emits a dirty
guitar riff until

the symmetrical stoicism
of her face is marred as she
cocks one brow, strongly hints
I should leave.

The bird's message:
U CAN'T MAKE BUNNY-EAR AIR QUOTES WITH UR MITTS ON NO ONE
KNOWS WHAT URE SAYING YUV GOTTA PEEL EM OFF

As if I'm the one
who's got razor sharps.
As if my mitts are a
pedantic pair of crows,
chasing a winter-starved
eagle away, back to the river,
squawking, *Stay off our campus.*
Use a semicolon.
Know your place.

And I keep my hands
covered because all I wanted
to say was that it's impossible
for this winter
to have gone on "too long."
That time's tactile
as a Slinky unfurling
between two six-year-olds
who just want
to get it all straight.
That spring starts
when spring starts.

All of which is not worth
the effort of baring palm
and knuckle to the elements.

So I bury my hands
in my pockets. They've
seen their shadows. They'll
keep a few more weeks.

How to Invoke the Patron Saint of Procrastination

St. Anti-Expeditusia

"O ye patroness of yo-yos, pinwheels,
handless watches, day planners martyred by burning,
cartwheelers, crabwalkers, patroness of lighters
of copious numbers of candles—

o ye glitterer of paper, crafty, o ye of
needless culinary quests, spreading homemade
brandy butter on homemade plum pudding,
oh ye brewer of tea, knitter of cozy,

ah blessed midnight organizer
of books and journals by alphabet,
by genre, by country of publication,
by size and year, by mood,

o ye of catnapping, roundabout inspiration,
ye chooser of stillness before action,
rushing at the end, your mind and stomach
teeming with startled fauns,

we've brought images of you braiding
and unbraiding your shambolic hair,
of you blowing Hubba Bubba bubbles
the size of your holy head,

oh please, please grant us guidance
by ensuring that whatever we've promised
to complete is accomplished,
ah let us eventually disappoint no one."

Every Dusk, Mothertongue.
Mothertonguing Every Dusk.

So you want to be a companion of the streets, my son, even the sea caves and creeks where the water is soused with disease. Your father was a caterwauling tomcat, with a chunk cut from one ear. He could hear the wind change, even when it blew soft; I could only hear his rapid heartbeat. How your father's heart thumped! I never forgave him, but I'll forgive you for leaving. Sons leave. Seasons change. The sea is a different sea every day. Always, when I taste bitter and underripe fruit, I will think of you, my son.

I will think of you, my son, always. When I taste bitter and underripe fruit, seasons change. Every day I see the sea differently, so you are forgiven and should leave. Please, leave; harken your own thumping heart. I never forgave your father when his began to blow soft, could only hear his old rapid beat. But he heard the wind change, even with a chunk cut from one ear. Your father was a tomcat too, caterwauling soused in diseased water, those sea caves and creeks. You and the streets are companions of want, my son.

Out(r)age

It is easier to find men who will volunteer
to die,
than to find those who are willing to endure pain
with patience.
                    —Julius Caesar

Right leg. You've done it this time. Across
the horse track's

gritty parking lot, pinched pain scorching
down joints

to the ankle so that I have to drag, like Kevin Spacey does
in *The Usual Suspects*.

My half-truncated gait pushes loose stones around,
such a tough guy,

despite its meek and gormless exterior. All the privileges
I gave you, righty:

kickball home runs, first step-offs at each crosswalk,
each stair,

even letting you always rest your more muscled self
atop lefty. Cain

smothering Abel—now more able than you!
And around in circles—

like I would walk now if I didn't correct myself,
one painful

lurch at a time—a horse gallops, lampoons me,
rhythmic

and metered: an echo of this afternoon's
hard-as-knuckle-duster

rain. The power's failed from storm or heat. Horses
stare callous-eyed

from their stalls. The stable doors slung open,
some with ropes

slackly stretching across. No dance-club bouncer here,
but the humidity

making us all sweat. And look at him: a harness
racer rings the track,

whip grasped like a fly-fishing rod, tipped up
so the leather

jangles loose. Showing off in denim
instead

of racing silk. Too muggy for frippery.
At home

the power's back on. Loneliness of the newscaster
sounding-off

on the awakened TV; the fridge vibrates, making up
for lost time.

Unsettled, penne and spaghettini rattle, like finks,
in high-placed canisters,

magnets threaten to dislodge themselves, to spill all
their secrets onto vinyl tiles.

TRAPPINGS

Hold your tempo and bless this house.

When I stop craving wild ginger
and a sky dense with pollen, I forget
the bees and their busy communion,
the Jack pines and the sea.

*

Briny drafts shrink these rooms,
spoil salt fish and meat,
potatoes from the cellar.
Mouthfuls of brackish wool:
mittens and scarves
laid out to dry on the radiator.

In spring we'll try to air ourselves out—
snap rhubarb stalks from black soil—
and dredge up how we look in sharper light.

*

Last night I dreamt about pitting pin cherries.
I laid the stones in a row on the table,
tossed ripe flesh into a bag under the sink,
and sensed you were gone.

You have run off, again;
I'll abandon these sweet things 'til you return.

Renters in pyjamas

embrace stout cats in discontented
huddles, while kids sleepily lean
against fleece-covered legs.

Word spreads of an actual fire,
not another false alarm
choked out by thirty years of dust,
from carpet being slowly
replaced, floor by floor, but
someone deep-frying while drunk.
Black smoke of peanut oil catching.
Smug cabinets bursting into flame
like they'd planned this auto-da-fé all along.

Patience—a rolled up pant cuff
coming loose—soaks up dew.

A medley of cellphones dial
to awaken lazy non-worriers,
non-insomniacs, to haul them
from between their sheets
and down cement stairways
that smell like old and fresh piss.
To lure them to the promise of drama,
the tale that'll be bandied beside
the mailboxes for a few weeks.

Silence ascends like hose-mist
as latecomers trickle out
from emergency exits.
Others try to guess the guilty party
who may be among them:
Anyone wobbly or standing alone.
Trying to catch a whiff of booze fume, of char.

The foreman with the grey handlebar
moustache no longer chats
with the super. Instead his ear's
stuck to his radio like he's
waiting for his jackpot number
to be called, for his life to finally
be different. A cottage on Kennebecasis,
an all-the-trimmings Ford F-250
with fast-action heated-seats
and rear-view mirrors that defrost
without being scraped. He answers
with a voice that's mostly rasp.
An asbestos-coated cough, structurally unsound,
like the ceiling finally collapsing.

A Millennial's Poem

Once a good deed per week
was enough to keep the world
on its Easy-Bake™ axis.
A 100-watt light bulb
and we can chew-goo
through this together.
Now I'm not so sure how to tally
and what goes in the column
that adds up to me being a good person.
Here's a youthful narrative
and a roll of Fruit by the Foot™.
I've gnawed on both
but only one bruised my tongue
Grimace™-purple. Here I am
grimacing, letting slip
my slap-bracelet age. Devil
Sticks™. Skip-It™. Stack of
timeworn *Tiger Beat*s.
I too am old enough to have once been
a magazine subscriber, to have once
hoarded Pogs™ in a fanny pack.
Grandfather galaxies untraded
before the bottom fell out
of the schoolyard marble market.
Lodestone, what an attractive economy
hardened from left-out Play-Doh™.
I'll trade you my TV memories
of hockey pucks lit-up in ice-dense USA,
you hand over the future
and whatever ease middle age
garnered you. Bargain
basement, *Top of the Pops*,

holy shit, you'll not believe
what I haven't had a chance
to have lost.

In my dreams I am always saying
goodbye and riding away
　　　　—Stevie Smith, "In My Dreams"

WESTWARD U-HAUL GOTHIC

b/c we've no CD player though we packed CDs
b/c I'm being driven through Manitoba in a Benadryl haze
b/c Manitoba goes on and on in its miraculous flatness
b/c despite the flatness I keep thinking of Brontë's moors
b/c the wind shunts the U-Haul like poor dramatic structure—the
    rising action of open fields, the falling action of windbreaks
b/c the climax of rumble strips
b/c near Portage la Prairie a black oil-train that is Heathcliff is about
    to take the dangerous turn that is Catherine
b/c the train takes the turn murderously slow and keeps going
b/c the plot that is Heathcliff leaves but can't actually leave the
    moment that is Catherine behind
b/c the rest is straight tracks and bad music
b/c a late spring storm coats the side-view mirror in ice and the
    prairies behind us are muddled
b/c at Gladstone's Happy Rock the crows are bullied by magpies
b/c I can't remember why smaller birds hate crows
b/c the crows are now Heathcliff
b/c at the Saskatchewan border the clouds clear
b/c here I don't know what Catherine is, maybe the ice melting,
    maybe remembering that there was ice
b/c all day the crows have a hard time of it
b/c a boat unzips a river and I don't know which river it is
b/c twenty-eight crows decide size is of little help and must rely on
    guile
b/c when they're not flying, the magpies wear white tank-tops
b/c Saskatchewan, up here, is not so flat and has more trees
b/c this is not how I pictured it, these rolling hills, a horizon
    comprehensible

b/c driving west into the sun feels too deliberate
b/c in the evening light the telephone lines are white spider silk
b/c ah, the never unfiltered voice of Catherine runs through those
    lines that are slowly becoming obsolete

Sand dunes. Dunes upon dunes. A vast tooth-colored superdune in the forgotten crook of the wasted West.
—Claire Vaye Watkins, *Gold Fame Citrus*

Spit's all that's holding me together.

Give me a small town not a rat-bit city scared by scarcity. Know your neighbour. Her weakness, his hiding spots. Whether you could see 'em thrown and still trust 'em. Blood may be thicker than water, but it's thinner than sand rain-pummelled to silt. In a pinch you can build a house with that.

Don't you go at it like a feral cat. Your hoard? *Hah!* There's hordes can tear through the side of a trailer like a kid through caramel.

That noise? A cricket with a bullhorn. A yodeller trapped in a mine shaft. The wind. Never stops, only kicks up when the clockwork gale dances like a drunk widow, shows her knickers, tells the whole lot of us to suck her marbles.

Wish you were stone deaf like that one cousin of yours? That's ears-down the silliest thing I ever half-heard. Clean that grit from your canals and who knows what'll slip past the keening.

Case in point. Last week, gossip fluttered mouth to ear, ear to mouth, our proverbial grapevine sprouting a ripe gobbet: that there's Old Randall dead in a cellar, hiding from the dust he became. Around him all these unshared cans. Beans, beans, beans. Tuna and smoked oysters. Seltzer water going flat in plastic. But *damn!* Them sacks of sugar stacked to the rafters. We all found ourselves scurrying like ants, like giant reckless ants.

Mandible-man, I see your mouth watering enough to puddle round your shoes. Bet you that tonight your dreams are of blood that's sweeter and wetter than the stories of Texans are large.

*Them!, 1954

44

WE DON'T DO ANYTHING RIGHT NOW.

Two minutes to bolt. Step lizard-light through the thin vibrations; my mother said, *Don't*. But that didn't help. So take time to pogo along the dune-street, up and down like a Western city's prospects. Here we're all a ghost town waiting to sun-bleach. Cracked no-name denim. Uneven bangs obscuring our eyes. Gotta keep that sun-bitch out somehow. Never know what we'll see when our veins are beef jerky hung on a phone pole.

There used to be a river run through here.

Hey, what plan can you enact when the ground is full of wet mouths, when you dream of wet mouths, and those mouths stink like a scared-dead polecat. With any luck a rocky outcropping can be salvation. The only moisture is that which is sheathed in goatskin. Canyon-eyes, what'd they eat before we got stuck here? *Greens*, he replies, *all the greens*.

Tremors, 1990

WATER'S PRECIOUS. SOMETIMES MAY BE MORE
PRECIOUS THAN GOLD.

My grandpa was one of them dowsers, well not really. He'd say, for
the best water-mining outfit, you only need three men. Anyone else
shows up you gotta kill. Keepers in lighthouses knew this. The three
part, not necessarily the killing. Need someone to report whether
rogue waves or bitterness built up over months did the deed. Rarer
for two to turn on one.

Know what a lighthouse is? Neither did I. But Grandpa said where
the water—great sheets of it—is jeopardous, people built towers so
their ships wouldn't gouge underneath. Hired men to spit light out
the way we do spines from poorly shucked Cholla buds. All year
looking out at grey water, grey sky. Rain dropping like what I can't
imagine. *Weeks of rain!* he said.

But out there on the dowsing trail, a stranger is a razor blade to the
throat, a hole in a water bag. The crew'd split and drink what they'd
find to keep from frothing like a mule bit by a rabid bat, 'til they'd score
an underground stream that was still clean. Something beyond moist.
Money in their wallets so serious it borders on stoic. Won't never crack
a smile, let alone make a joke of 'em.

Most didn't find nothing, not that they were supposed to, came back
with tongues of desperate parchment, only water they'd imagined
turning to mud and grit that they'd scoop up anyway; beggars can't
be choosy when their eyes no longer cry, not a drop to spare. Dew-
brains, the lot of 'em. Scores of trios scouring a place dryer and dryer
'til they were just grit on the wind blown someplace better, or so
my grandpa'd say, having sold them some map or other, some tale
to rein in a thirst that they couldn't remember not having. His cut
already poured in his canteen and pissed away. And him already off to

another town when some raisined rube got wise to his scheme. Sure, yeah, my grandpa knew how to keep his water bags full.

*The Treasure of the Sierra Madre, 1948

No MAN NEEDS NOTHING.

Supply lines, railroad tracks blasted to hyphens. When is a line no longer a line, but a message in Morse code: a dune is a bosom that can't be suckled on.

So turn to lightweight fabrics, a trustworthy weave that the wind speaks through. Sure once you were towheaded blond, but now all blond is sun-corrupted white, all blue eyes, bluer next to tan beyond burn. Sunspots. Djinn hovering in seared retina. Near to pure prophesy as a white man glimpses in the desert.

Real portending comes later, after tunnel vision. Mouth of boy who is sand-swallowed. Better to swerve into the new future, a flame that still hurts, though some can pretend. Oh never-beloved, bastard-son, spin around like a lone particle in a sandstorm.

It's amazing how mislaid a soldier can get. Useful as a gun held to a temple.

Lawrence of Arabia, 1962

Now pick up what you can and run.

Desperate to fashion a duck's back; no water to slide off of it. Rivers are steps down and steps up from even ground. A whole space left beyond, below beleaguered, space shaped like what? Like the underneath of tables. A stuck citrus segment of a revolving door. A space in the shape of our mothers, in the shape of their unpaid work. So we skipped learning gracefulness, bargaining up to holy grace instead: a twenty-month-old toothbrush, bristles angled, teeth of crocodiles, akimbo down to my silly socks, my ringless fingers. Clown-heart, let's all laugh at your greasepaint frown and pantomimic gestures. Call me your ever-entwined droopy-eyed philistine. Call me such a mouthful. There's this desert spreading farther and faster than thought. Synaptic sidewinder. Tongue coated in cinnamon. When the wind shuts its eerie trap, you can hear yourself blink. Even the beautiful young aren't sure about mercy.

*Mad Max: Fury Road, 2015

Avoiding East-Coast Nostalgia Out West

*I'm learning
the eddies, the tug of my new city, new magpies.*
        —Jessica Hiemstra

So I'd forgotten the sound of birds. Bingo lady
magpies griping because their squares
are bare. Pigeons landing like bad apologies
on the balcony above mine. I imagine delicate coos

while they angle their heads: dun-coloured
sociopaths, all Hannibal Lecter cocking an ear
for hot pot offal of oil patch worker.
Wheat-farmer sirloin in semi-demi-glace.

And the sun for days and days, such persistence,
curtain tattooing the bedspread with laced shadow.
No spring storm coming in, no nor'easter to bend the branches,
to litter sidewalks with tree buds. Readjustment

be damned. Don't let me miss mist-rain that can't be stopped
by slicker or umbrella. Or the busker calling out
POEM FOR A PENNY! who threatens when declined:
Fuck you, you scarf-wearing bitch.

But the birds each morning keep singing
with nothing yet to be done. So every day
I cozy up to the balcony as I Wi-Fi my resumé
for jobs that actually pay. And practise my

you-can-trust-me smile, secretly wiping nerve-sweat
palms along my good dress pants before gripping.
And I practise my song for student loan repayment,
my not-so-soft landing, feathered somehow new.

ONE THING — THEN ANOTHER

the sun isolates me

> my ADD surfacing
> like a farmer's tan

look at the way the Western light
makes an embossed riddle
of that woman's black hair

> every moment falling
> in and out of distraction

and the way the shadow
from that new hotel
is the sail of a Spinosaurus
cresting across Jasper Avenue—

> minutia, lovely
> detritus of the sparked eye

> 'til I'm dizzy-drunk
> and lonely, need
> boundaries, limits,
> darkness

so I duck into a bar,
a faux dive:
no greasy heads
but enough product
that I feel my fingers
stick together in sympathy

and I want to stay here
hidden among the band's single
and double stroke rolls
among denim-clad nodders
'til the sun falls
down the stairs, through
a plate glass window;
stay until he nurses
his pride and injuries
at home, half-broken,
with a suitably unmoved
woman asking *how exactly
did* this *happen?*

hey, barkeep, pour me a drink
tell me your name,
your story, what's worth
telling—if your dreams
have words, tell me those too.

Nobody Every Day Keeps Saying Nothing

i)

But here's to the dogs' barking protest
at the day too warm for December,

got their dander up,
chucking themselves

at drab fences like rage zombies.
If a butterfly's doily wings

once prompted a riot of windstorm
in wherever,

each overheated dog's breath
could be the mass migration of us all.

And tonight I'll wonder
if that canine ruckus

was the right-cross that shined
the moon's eye with ice-crystal halo

for the last time.

ii)

"For the last time" is now
our mantra: for the last time,

this weather cannot hold
us. Or we cannot hold on,

not even 'til the PEI-sized asteroid
that we were promised

kicks off a new impact winter.
For my impossible grandchildren:

the sub-zero you'll never know
was a cold steak pulled from the freezer

placed on swelling. So that now
all you'll have to eat is flesh-defrosted air.

How Turkeys Become City-Dwellers in Edmonton

They stub their turkey toes on the uneven ledge of
the light-rail-car door, yet still remember to sit facing
the direction the train is running, to hold backpack
on lap, to pull into self and not take up space that
should be theirs, while testing for broken talon, for
bruised ego.

They learn grates are slippery in the dew, deadly
in the winter. None of Marilyn's flirtatious panty
slip, hot air shooting her skirt up like tail-feathers
in a mating ritual. Just the gut laugh of sprawling
game, torqued slapstick wings, a pillow-fight moult
layering rush hour.

They help a cyclist to the ground after he takes a
hasty turn into a sedan, still standing, weaving
like a yearling pine in a nor'easter. Hold a wing to
his scalp 'til the ambulance and cops come. Leave
before answering questions, blood on feather, blood
on breast. No one noticing the blood on them as
they walk home.

They're complimented for their wild-turkey style
by a homeless woman under-clad in November:
her spaghetti straps, jean skirt, blue lips, goose—
not turkey—bumps. Really they feel they've been
wearing their second-best outfits since hatching.
The magpies shaming them with clean lines, with
iridescence.

They give coins, stop; give eye contact, stop; give silence. Hold their wishbones inside for something to change, to better.

They sure don't know that no one thanks the bus driver, then they know but do it anyway, feel made for thanksgiving. Warble it over diesel engine rumble.

They forget, even in the rare rain, to crick their turkey necks at building height, no longer risk apocryphal drowning, grow used to the vertical plane.

They see how others wrap their wattles in jewel-toned fabrics, the strangers swathed in luxury while wearing leaky shoes. The turkeys buy their own pairs, then buy an array of seasonally inappropriate pashminas on sale. Next year, after twelve months of high rents, they'll learn impracticality, let their shoes fall to dusty pieces, their scarves a tapestry, delicate embroidery revealing what is valued, what isn't.

Steady Work if You Can Get It

The prairie wind takes a day job,
slapbrush stuccoes the river.

The river is the wind's ceiling
and the sun and the moon,

for him, are the same light
calibrated to a different brightness.

His coveralls are mostly dust.
His steel toes could kick

the warmth right out of you.
His favourite trowel too, comes from

the north and has sharp edges
that catch. That he leaves a mess

behind him and can't be found
are not faults: plasterers

are an enigma who gust in and out,
must be dogged. The slipshod wind

lives for the moment, always.
He doesn't know how to stop.

Boyle Street Triptych

i.

Plastic-wrapped mattress portage
      along 95TH Street. The crick in the carrier's neck,
         his eyeline blocked, the vertical
            imagined. What wished for rocky outcrops
    and runty, rain-starved trees? What stars
pockmarking, what degree of moon?

ii.

Gritty air. Back lanes unpaved. Rut of shopping trolley.
Can-pickers in bins, dust covered, in their beards,
on their dried-sweat-hardened jeans, their shoes
cracked and coated: rimed archeologists
discovering their own graves.

iii.

Nearby, the other CN Tower, less ~~ugly~~ impressive,
a decked-out aging mod, vertical stripes
for what used to be a lean flank, at night
red-eyed and circling his name, looking
for a booker, a manager, someone to remember
how tall he used to be.

D$_2$O

A friend is losing his soul three time zones away. I don't even believe in souls, but he's losing something. He lives within a dampness that keeps people sodden and secure, reasonable. Like their innards, what's outside their bodies is mostly water, so they can't forget where they came from. I went to grade school near a CANDU nuke plant and at twelve learned of heavy water. Can't remember anything about it now, just that some water at atomic-scale must be easier to carry than others. Where my friend calls home, cars all fall to pieces from salt and rain, and here they keep going light as empty water skins. Could take off from one side of the river and land with a cloud of rust on the other. Their chassis sloughed to bird-bone. But my friend feels heavier without his soul, that I can't think of another word for, his not-soul soul. Like some nemesis hated emptiness so spat on a sadiron and sutured it inside him. Now he's a pulp and paper mill burning down near the dank earth, which is too far away in a country that's too big to be of any help.

A March Commuter Considers Newton's Third Law

Foot-drenched as the cars
swoop past. City of trucks
souped-up, wide-stanced,
manspreading axles.

When it rains, I want
to be each car skimming
along, tires hurling
bursts behind them
as if fallen water
wants to become cloud again.

It is still in me to desire
to be a thing displacing.

Next rare rain, I'll see myself
as water forced that courses
over the curb and sidewalk,
then lulls thin, evaporates,
a puddle that is moved on.

It is not enough,
this existence as a droplet in the air,
form changed, vapour
dispersed, my molecules
drifting further in the prairie wind.

We're always nailed to our atoms,
our momentums, our impacts on others.
Always will be.

*

Striding past the bus shelter,
a lanky lad asks his doppelgänger:
So you'd take a vampire's life?

Though I don't hear who kills
and who is killed,
I see how the question
lands on the look-alike friend: saucer-eyed surprise
at one concept but not necessarily the other.

Concept A: One man clutches
the stake and plants it
in the chest of the undead,
rescinding a life grown too long in the tooth.

Concept B: One man willingly wears undeath
and plunges his teeth into the pulse of another,
the smell of pennies, bowels giving out
as he devours.

My bus arrives with squealing breaks
and a door that needs oiling.
I will never know if one man was considering
whether he would consume another
or end another's all consuming consumption.

*

How about that boy I heard exclaim
about gorillas riding on the bus
and only monkeys in the cars? He would now
be in high school, nearly graduated.
Would have an iPhone, follow favourite YouTube stars
like he's a small ship, like they keep him
on a route to riches or escape,
not dead-reckoned in a job he hates.

How about my mum, always telling me
that in just over 100 years, everyone
on Earth will be dead, so not to worry
about what little thing I did or said?
Even that gorilla boy: dead. So here I am
on another bus with thirty-three strangers
who'll eventually be forgotten too.

*

The sedan dodges the bus,
nearly merging into the hinge
that separates the two compartments.

Bulging, panicked-horse eyes of the man
at the wheel of the sedan. He treads sharp
hooves alongside a massasauga rattler.

The oblivious bus driver surges forth.
The car just stops right in time. No one but me
in the back compartment sees the near collision.

Both vehicles cross the river, one driver shaken,
the bridge's sturdy bars too much
a comfort, the sky cowering too close.

*

No one swims in the river
no matter how turquoise it runs
Still, it can be counted upon,
and only floods the three
predictable neighbourhoods
built well after the terrible deluge of 1915,
when houses were banned for many years
in the valley. How about
losing everything twice—
the water seeping and dragging away
and the laws saying never
to return. At least not until
memory dries out in the sun.
A law that always forces
away and bequeaths land or land-
lessness on those it spills upon,
overflowing, the banks ever-shifting.
Some to protect, some not.
So the flood-crossed were settled
like teacups on a shelf,
out of a danger they thought
was theirs alone.

HER PILLOW SMELLS OF THE SPECIAL

The fruity jazz is a silly titter
when it should be Ella Fitzgerald
mourning corrupted love, a voice
that slit a million hearts and dared them
to keep beating. The waitress carries away
Friday-night detritus, citrus slices
pierced by straw pikes, puddling ice,
napkins warped by clutch.

Her fears are fallen arches, spider veins
web-marring her seamless legs
as she maneuvers past customers,
their steep leans against the bar's copper top.
When they topple she'll ask them to leave,
turning sloppy geometry into sloppy kinetics.

Her colouring matches the art:
an exploded poppy, a ginger man,
his beard parting the slate grey sky.

She so-adroitly ministers a Sazerac,
an amber iris diffracting across the pine table.
Tonight she'll dream again
of rows of taps, of rows
of taps, of rows of taps.

THE THERE, THERE, THERE

For Rob

There, a man down-the-hatches Jägerbombs.
His berserker shriek silent
like it would be in outer space.
The punk band's pulsations and oscillations—
sound-checking to oblivion—push the room
over capacity with bass and screech. No leeway
for anyone else. Small-talk, love-talk, just plain-talk
jettisoned, weightless debris unlikely to be noted.

There, human forms of binary stars pull
toward their shared centre of mass. From afar
they're Siamese twins: a single body,
double bright. Unable to lose themselves
to a beat that isn't their own counterweight swinging,
they lean into each other's headspace to concoct
pub names: *The Roving Lander, The Supernova
and Tan-line, The Mislaid Astronaut.*

There, the bartender adjusts her strapless dress
while filling a pitcher, scoops the foam, yanks,
fills the rest. Amps her smile and orbits back,
sloshing her wares as if tonight's the perigean
spring tide. Round and round all shift,
'til her last-call smile is the comet that'll soon
clout the Earth into impact winter: *Yeah, you may not
have a home to go to, but you can't stay here.*

My Grade Six Meteorology Lessons Help Me Categorize Pedestrians

Summer lovers of wheels whip on by,
Cirrus-wisp-of-youth, coltish, hot airbursts
from nostrils, the sweat whisking from their rosed-up
faces, heavenward like pure thoughts.
Neon on denim flaring by and away,
chit-chatting over each other like no one
can hear them—
                    which I can't really—
half a sentence and they're
gone, no blistery message pulsing me in my place
'til I miss summer, miss too-hot wind,
miss each one of my sizzling past selves.

More swift ones swoop beyond with gusty strides,
but in neutral disguise, wrinkleless black, navy, grey—
no flashy purple or sick sleet-green,
no totter to their posture. Places to go,
colleagues to sway, Nimbostrategic-climber,
with paper in paperclips, highlighters beaconing
the points they'll forecast.
                          On their feet, not runners
but weatherproofed leather spit-shone,
another beacon to cut through what
could be a sodden year. Though they're sure
the flowers grow thanks to them, fair days
are for the weak, won't sit on a subway seat,
but always take the stairs, always taking
notice.

A certain silhouette:
mole hunch to shoulders,
like they're unexpectedly aboveground
and must watch their feet,
a Cumulonimbovagabond shambling down the street.
Too many of them to count. Our neighbourhood spits them out like
  hail:
          pitter-patter spittle of pebbled ice
that we avoid, taking shelter from the reverse-lure
of sadness multiplied with deprivation to flat vapour
that builds into a struck cloud-anvil and spills: lightning, torrents,
bulky thunder that makes me jump. Don't throw salt down, just grit,
          'til I look away,
pass them passed out in backlanes, in greenspace,
empty lots. What a terrible moment to be hit
by a simple bolt from the sky. How weathered.
How understandably escaped from self
through sudden motion,
                              know I'd do it too
if I was out in all seasons, a sheer force
knocking down signs, mailboxes, booting parked cars,
ditching ruined shoes, bellowing 'til the damn-of-it-all
splits me unconscious and the clear sky
that isn't me prevails.

Turtles All the Way Down

Frost whittles the edges off, a pill popped
to alleviate too-loud leaves.
But it doesn't spread ease.

A crash on an arterial route for the third time this week.
And for the second time, the girl woke from scantron dreams
where she graphites in C – C – C – C
all the way down
like that old anecdote about turtles.

When she learns turtles don't hibernate
but wait immobile underwater,
attuned to light that will let them know
when to scurry back to melting life,
she gains new respect for hard shells
clasped in slurry below hard ice.
At the same time, she thinks
turtles must taste fantastic to have shells like that,
like lobsters, like coconuts and walnuts,
like every hard thing that must be cracked
open. This is the first time she hungers
for a creature she respects.

Cars still as living statues in November.
Chilled breath. Exhaust.

She is passed by other poor test-takers,
who were up at dawn, getting at 'er.
Muscles already warmed by hours of work.
Their open jackets flapping with speed
that they concoct from coffee and will.
Compared to them she is hibernating.
And she doesn't even like coffee,
is sure she lent her will to her best friend
who forgot to give it back after growing beyond
needing a backup. Her surplus will heaped
in a hometown closet with Troll Doll
and mood ring, with Dream Phone phone.

The podgy magpies, winter feathers in earlier
than last year, with more energy than meteors,
dip and pluck frozen-deep-fried-now-refrozen french fries.

A girl slow as purple slush in a Slurpee machine.
No means to hold her breath until spring,
to slacken her blood. No means to bolt about,
to kick away the snow and dredge up
some edible *amuse-bouche*. No means to fly it off,
a prize garnish placed on peppy survival.

This morning she discovered her leather gloves
no longer fit. But there's a solid edge between
her un-shelled skin and the quill-prick cold.
Warm-blooded, she wants to lash out at the stuck cars
and their cocky ownership of this city.

She thinks, *Anything could, and does happen.*
Eventually.

The epigraph for "EAST" is from Karen Solie's poem "Bitumen" from her book *The Road In Is Not the Same Road Out*, published by House of Anansi Press, 2015.

"Cool Enough to Sink a Ship" refers to Patti Smith's cover of "Hey Joe," the A-side to her 1974 single on MER Records. This poem is for Kayla Geitzler.

The title "Tick, Tick, Tick Went the Machine in the Bushes" is from Virginia Woolf's last novel, *Between the Acts*. The poem also uses a line by Algernon Charles Swinburne's "Hymn to Proserpine": "the world is not sweet in the end."

"A Millennial Poem" references Fox TV's bizarre decision to have a glowing puck for hockey games so that Americans could follow the game.

The epigraph for "THEN" is from *All the Poems: Stevie Smith*, published by New Directions, 2016.

The epigraph for "WEST" is from Claire Vaye Watkins's novel *Gold Fame Citrus*, published by Riverhead Books, 2015.

The titles from "The Land of Cinematic Drought" are from movies whose main setting is desert. Images in the poems are also inspired by images in those films.

The epigraph for "Avoiding East-Coast Nostalgia Out West" is from Jessica Hiemstra's poem "A new country is learning small creatures, the cornflowers" from her collection *Apologetic for Joy*, published by Goose Lane Editions, 2011.

"How Turkeys Become City-Dwellers in Edmonton" was inspired by a tweet, "How New England Turkeys Became City Dwellers," promoting Yoni Appelbaum's *The Atlantic* article, "Why Wild Turkeys Hate the Wild," published online on November 25, 2015.

"Boyle Street Triptych" references Edmonton's CN Tower, which was the tallest building in Western Canada for five years (1966–1971). At the time of writing, it had fallen to lucky number thirteen in the Edmonton rankings.

"Nobody Every Day Keeps Saying Nothing" describes the fact that ice crystals in the atmosphere are said to cause halos around the moon, though this is debated.

D_2O is the chemical symbol for heavy water, which is used to do something in CANDU reactors.

Newton's Third Law of Motion, from "A March Commuter Considers Newton's Third Law," is the mathematical principle that "when one body exerts a force on a second body, the second body simultaneously exerts a force equal in magnitude and opposite in direction on the first body."

"Turtles All the Way Down" is for Brittany Lauton, who still has a Dream Phone phone.

Acknowledgements

Thank you to the editors of the following journals for publishing earlier versions of poems from this book: *FreeFall Magazine, Poetry is Dead, Arc, Prairie Fire, The Literary Review of Canada, CV2,* and *The Minola Review.*

Thanks to Fredericton and Edmonton, two places where I've made a home as an adult. Thanks to those who made me feel welcome in these two weird and beautiful cities. And thanks to everyone who helped me wrangle with these poems: Martin Ainsley, John Barton, Leah Faieta, Michael Jessome, Brittany Lauton, Ross Leckie, Ian LeTourneau, Mike Meagher, Rob Ross, Rebecca Salazar, and Sue Sinclair.

Thanks to everyone at ECW. You are all top notch.

To my mum, who supported me moving so far away (twice!) to study and write poetry.

To Rob Ross, who has my heart and my back.